# Introduction

This is the story of the greatest center in basketball today: Kareem Abdul Jabbar of the Milwaukee Bucks. His great height and quick moves have made him a winner since he was a teen-ager. Playing under the name his parents gave him—Lew Alcindor—he led his high school team to the Catholic School championship of New York City. In college he led the UCLA Bruins to three straight national championships. And in only his second year at Milwaukee the seven-foot two-inch center carried the Bucks to the professional basketball championship of the world.

It is also the story of a young black man whose deepening understanding of himself led him to change his religion and, finally, to change his name.

## Sports Hero

# KAREEM ABDUL JABBAR
## The Story of Lew Alcindor

by Marshall and Sue Burchard

G. P. Putnam's Sons  •  New York

PHOTO CREDITS
Marshall and Sue Burchard, p. 17
Tom Zuk, pp. 13, 15
United Press International, pp. 2, 32, 34, 40, 43, 49, 51, 56, 58, 61, 65, 68, 71, 76, 79, 83, 86, 89, 90, 91, 94, 98, 102, 109, 110
*Illustrations by Paul Frame.*

**Fifth Impression**

Copyright © 1972 by Marshall and Sue Burchard
All rights reserved. Published simultaneously
in Canada by Longmans Canada Limited, Toronto.
**SBN: GB-399-60699-8**
**SBN: TR-399-20284-6**
Library of Congress Catalog Card Number: 72-181324
PRINTED IN THE UNITED STATES OF AMERICA
07210

# Contents

# 1

# Boy from New York City

Ferdinand Lewis Alcindor, Jr., was born on April 16, 1947, in New York City. At his birth he was almost 2 feet long. He weighed nearly 13 pounds. Very few babies are that big when they are born.

Height ran in the Alcindor family. Young Lew's mother was

nearly 6 feet tall. His father was almost 6 feet 3 inches. Lew's grandfather was bigger still. He stood 6 feet 8 inches.

Lew's grandparents came from an island in the Caribbean Sea. The name of the island is Trinidad. It is just off the coast of South America. There is a road in Trinidad named after the Alcindors.

Lew was very proud of his grandparents. They spoke several languages. His grandfather spoke English and Yoruba, an African language. His grandmother spoke English, Spanish, French, and the language of Trinidad.

When Lew was a little boy, the Alcindors lived in the part of New York City called Harlem. They lived in an apartment house that was only one block from Central Park. Lew's mother took him to the park to play.

The Alcindor home was full of music. Lew's parents met when they were singing in a church choir. They taught him to love all kinds of music. His favorite was jazz.

When Lew was five years old, his father graduated from a famous New York music school, the Juilliard School of Music. This was an important event for the Alcindor family. Lew's grandparents and many other relatives came for the graduation. After the ceremony, the new graduates played their instruments. It made Lew proud to see his father playing his trombone with the other graduates.

Lew's father had studied how to be a conductor of an orchestra. But when he went to look for a

job, he couldn't find an orchestra
that would hire a black conductor.
Since he couldn't get a job doing

what he really wanted to do, Mr. Alcindor went to work for a furniture company. Later he became a transit policeman. A transit policeman protects people riding on buses and subways.

Mr. Alcindor never forgot about his music. Sometimes he took Lew with him to the Elks Club in Harlem, where he played with other musicians just for fun. Famous jazz musicians like Dizzy Gillespie played there, too.

The Alcindors moved out of Harlem when Lew was still a young boy. His father didn't like the way the neighborhood was changing. It was becoming crowded and dirty. Mr. Alcindor wanted his family to have a nicer place to live.

Lew's Street in Harlem.

The Alcindors moved to a housing project in another part of New York City called Inwood. It was very different from living in Harlem. The buildings were bigger, but there was lots of green grass between them. Lew had many places to play.

The Alcindors lived in a tall apartment building with more than one hundred and fifty other families. The people who lived in the building came from all over the world. There were families from Cuba, England, Germany,

The Alcindor's building in Inwood.

Ireland, Puerto Rico and Russia. Their children all played together happily when they were small. The children didn't care if they had different-colored skins or if their parents had different religions.

When Lew was old enough for first grade, he went to a nearby school called St. Jude's. It was run by Catholic nuns.

There was only one other black student in the whole school, but that didn't matter to Lew. He got along well with everybody. He

learned to read quickly. He en-
joyed school. He spent three happy
years at St. Jude's.

Saint Jude's School

# 2

# Learning the Game

When Lew was ready for fourth grade, his parents sent him to a boarding school near Philadelphia. Both of his parents were working. There was nobody at home during the day to take care of him. The Alcindors thought Lew would be better off at boarding school.

The school was called Holy Providence. It was run by nuns just like St. Jude's. But the students were from a very different background from the ones at St. Jude's. Lew's classmates at Holy Providence were black children from the poor neighborhoods of Philadelphia, Baltimore, and Washington, D.C.

Lew had trouble making friends with them at first because he was a good reader and liked books. Most of his classmates could not read well.

The nuns were pleased that

Lew was a good reader. They asked him to read aloud to the seventh graders. The nuns said, "Listen to him. This is how you should read." The other students didn't like that. They thought Lew was strange for being such a good reader.

Then they took another look at him. He was only nine years old and a fourth grader, but he was the second tallest boy in the school. The school went up to eighth grade.

One of the older boys finally grabbed Lew one day and said, "Come on. We gonna teach you a game."

The game was basketball. Lew didn't know much about it. He had tried bouncing a basketball, but it always bounced away from him. Still the boys wanted him on the team because he was so tall.

They took him to a playground and taught him how to play. The playground had no regular basket, so the boys tied up a peach basket with the bottom cut out of it and used that instead. They played rough basketball.

Lew practiced at the playground a lot. But he didn't play in many games that year because he was four years younger than the other boys on the team. Still, from then on, the most important thing in his life was basketball.

The next year Lew did not go back to Holy Providence. Instead he stayed home and went back to St. Jude's for his fifth-grade year.

In the winter he went out for basketball. He was so tall that he made the eighth grade team. But he was growing so fast that he was having trouble making all the parts of his body work together smoothly. He moved a little awkwardly.

That summer, he went out for track. He learned to run fast. His speed soon came in handy. One day two boys tried to steal his English racing bike. They rode up on their own bikes, picked up Lew's, and rode off with it. Lew ran after them for two miles. The boys finally gave up, dropped the bike, and pedaled away as fast as they could.

By the time Lew entered the seventh grade he was 6 feet 5

inches tall and still growing fast. Much of his earlier awkwardness was gone. He was becoming a very good basketball player.

One day something very exciting happened. He jumped up to shoot a basket. He touched the rim! He had never been able

to do that before. No one else on the team could come close to doing it.

It seemed almost too good to be true. Lew wanted to make sure he wasn't dreaming. When the game ended, he waited until the gym was empty and then he tried to do it again. Up he jumped, and again he touched the rim. He did it thirty times in a row before he stopped.

It was quite a trick and it made him a bit cocky. He began trying all kinds of other tricks like dribbling the ball behind his

back or shooting without looking at the basket. The other players tried tricky plays, too. Lew's good friend, the basketball coach, Farrell Hopkins, thought they were fooling around too much. He said it would be better if they worked harder on ordinary plays.

Lew entered the eighth grade. It was his last year at St. Jude's. He and his teammates wanted to win their league championship for Coach Hopkins. They won most of their games, but they still could not capture first place.

It was a good year for Lew. He

had grown another 3 inches and stood 6 feet 8 inches tall. The taller he grew, the easier it was for him to make baskets. In one game he scored 33 points.

Something else wonderful happened that year. He found that he could jump high enough so that he could actually stuff the ball down through the basket. He was only fourteen years old, but he could dunk a basketball like a pro!

# 3

# Tower of Power

Several high schools wanted Lew to come and play on their basketball teams. They sent recruiters to watch him play. The recruiters gave Lew free tickets to pro games. He got to meet some of his basketball heroes that way.

He finally decided to go to

Power Memorial Academy in the middle of New York City. It was supposed to be a good school. It was easy to reach by subway. Most important, Lew liked the Power basketball coach, Jack Donahue. Lew thought that the coach had a good sense of humor. He thought that playing for Coach Donahue would be fun.

Lew entered Power in the fall of 1961. The change of schools was difficult for him. The teachers at Power were very strict. They made him work very hard in class. The white students no longer seemed friendly. Lew realized that some of them did not like him simply because he was black. He spent a lot of time alone. He practiced basketball harder than ever.

Russian history class at Power

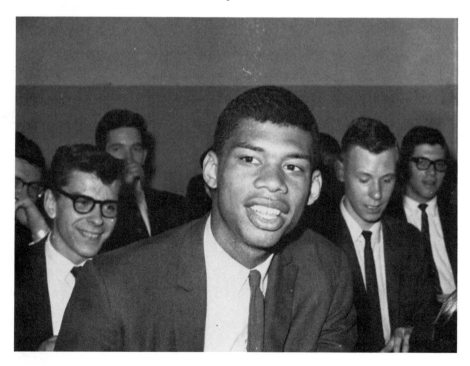

By his second year in high school he was old enough to play on the varsity team. His position was center. He soon showed that he was not only the biggest but also the best high school center in all of New York City. The other four players on the Power varsity were good, too. If another team tried to guard Lew too closely, he passed the ball over their heads to one of his teammates. Power went the whole season without losing a game. They were champions of the the city's Catholic school league.

Lew's dunk shot was unstoppable.

In Lew's third year at Power the basketball team kept right on winning. The teams they played tried everything to stop them. In one game Lew was leaning over a player to keep him from shooting. The boy he was guarding got so mad that he bit Lew's arm.

Coach Donahue was a successful coach. But in one game Lew found out that the coach cared more about winning than he did about his players' feelings.

Power was playing a team that should have been easy to defeat.

But Lew and his teammates played poorly, and at half time they were ahead by only three baskets. Between the halves, Coach Donahue spoke to his players in the locker room. He told each boy how badly he was playing. Pointing at Lew, the coach accused him of not trying hard enough.

"You're acting just like a nigger!" the coach said.

Lew was shocked. He didn't know what to do. A black friend on the team told him, "Go home, man, go home."

Another black teammate said, "Man, you can't go for that kind of talk! Go home!"

Lew started to follow their advice, but then he changed his mind. He played the second half and he played well. Power won the game.

After it was over, Coach Donahue asked Lew to come into his office. The coach smiled, put his arm around Lew, and said, "See? My plan worked. I knew that if I used that word it would shock you into playing a good second half."

Lew was furious. He was so mad that he was tempted to quit the team, and the school, at once. But he wanted to go on to a good college. So he kept his anger to himself and stayed in school.

That summer he went to work for an organization in Harlem called Haryou-Act. He was paid $30 a week, and he had a chance to attend a journalism workshop. He learned about putting out a newspaper. He learned about other things, too.

His teacher taught him a lot of African history. Lew had not known that seven hundred years ago there were important African civilizations in places like Ghana and Mali. He was fascinated. He read as much as he could about African history. He had always been proud of his parents and grandparents. Now he was proud of his ancestors, too.

One day at the end of the summer something happened that Lew would never forget. When he got off the subway train in Harlem, he walked straight into a terrible riot. It was a wild scene. People were smashing

store windows and stealing what-
ever they could. The police were
clubbing them with nightsticks
to stop them. There was even
some shooting.

Harlem riot.

Lew was terrified. He ran away as fast as he could. He ran until he was out of breath. Finally he stopped. He thought about what the riot meant. He could see that the poor black people of Harlem were very angry. He thought he understood why. They were tired of being poor and tired of being treated unfairly because they were black. He realized he was angry, too.

Lew was seventeen years old when he went back to Power for his final year of high school. That winter the basketball team lost one game. They won the New York City Catholic school championship for the third year in a row.

As a high school basketball player Lew had been a sensation. Over three seasons, he had scored a total of 2,067 points, which was a record for New York City high school players. His parents were proud and happy. Their famous son had been a good student as well as a great athlete. They knew he could get into just about any college he wanted.

Leaping high to
block a shot.

Holding high school
championship trophy.

# 4

# Off to California

Many colleges wanted Lew Alcindor for their basketball teams. They knew that whoever got him would have a championship team.

Lew thought very hard about where he wanted to go to college. Two schools interested him most. One was the University of California at Los Angeles, called

UCLA for short. The other was the University of Michigan.

In the spring of his last year in high school, the people at UCLA paid to have Lew fly out to Los Angeles to look over their campus. They went all out to impress him. He was met at the airport by one of the coaches and two black players from the basketball team. They showed him the journalism school, the new music building and the dormitories where the students lived.

Lew thought the campus was beautiful. He liked the people he met, too. They all told him what a great place UCLA was, and he believed them. He stayed for a whole week. Then he flew home and told his parents that he had decided to go to UCLA.

He left for California with mixed feelings. He was sorry to be moving away from his parents. But he was looking forward to life at UCLA. The riot in Harlem had helped give him a bad feeling about New York. He thought that things might be better out West. He thought that the people there respected each other and didn't care what color a man's skin was.

He soon learned differently. Things turned out to be pretty much the same for him at UCLA as they had been at the other schools he had attended. Most of the students were white. Some of them were unfriendly to him because he was black. Sometimes they made jokes about how tall he was. He liked being tall. It made him angry when people made fun of him.

He did make a few good friends. They were other black

athletes. They took him on long walks up into the mountains.

While they walked, they talked about their pride in being black. They discussed the teachings of Malcolm X and other black leaders they admired. Most of all they talked about the Islamic religion, the religion of many black people all over the world. Lew learned a lot from his new friends.

During the winter he played center on the freshman basketball team. There were several other really good players on the team. Together they were unbeatable.

Grabbing a rebound against the varsity.

They won their games so easily that they became a little bored. They won one game by 103 points. They even beat the UCLA varsity by 15 points. That was quite an accomplishment. The varsity had been national champions the year before.

Head coach John Wooden saw that Lew wasn't getting enough competition. He needed to be challenged by better players if he hoped to get better himself. The coach hired a graduate student named Jay Carty to work out with Lew. Jay was 6 feet 8

Coach Wooden giving Lew tips on shooting.

inches tall and was a great basketball player. He was very good at moving around the floor.

Lew and Jay played two-man games. Jay played roughly on purpose. He said Lew was too soft and needed toughening. Jay took a piece of chalk. He drew a line on the backboard a foot and a half above the rim. Every day Lew had to jump up and touch the line ten times with each hand. The exercise strengthened his legs so he could jump even higher than before.

# 5

# College Champions

When Lew went back to UCLA for his second year, he decided he didn't want to live in a dormitory. He thought some of the students he lived with his first year were silly. They didn't seem concerned with serious problems in the world. For fun they did things like flood the hallways and slide

53

around the floor on their bare behinds. Lew wasn't interested in that kind of fun. So he and another black basketball player, Edgar Lacey, took an apartment together.

Lew went out for the varsity. He and three other sophomores made the starting team. The fifth starter, Mike Warren, was a junior.

Everyone expected UCLA to win the national championship. But Lew and his teammates had their doubts. They knew they were a young team and would come up against some strong opposition. They practiced so hard getting ready for the season that they were almost worn out before the first game.

They opened the season against the University of Southern California. It was a big game for Lew. Sports fans all over the country were waiting to find out how he would do in his first varsity game. He felt nervous. All he had for dinner before the game was some tea and honey.

He wanted to be good. He was great. He scored on lay-ups,

hook shots, jump shots and dunks. He made 23 out of 32 shots. He also made 10 out of 14 free throws from the foul line.

Scoring against Southern California.

Altogether he scored 56 points and broke the UCLA scoring record in his very first varsity game. UCLA won the game by a score of 105–90.

Lew had been able to score freely because only one player was guarding him. UCLA's next opponent, Duke University, did not want to make the same mistake. So they sent in three big men to guard him. For seven and one-half minutes Lew couldn't even get off a shot.

He felt as if he were in jail. The arms and legs of the Duke men

Surrounded by Duke players.

surrounding him were like bars. But he knew what to do. He passed to his teammates who were in the open. They pumped the ball into the basket. Lew made only 19 points, but UCLA won the game easily by a score of 88–54.

After that UCLA settled into a pattern. Whenever another team guarded Lew too closely, he passed off to teammates like Lucius Allen, Ken Heitz and Lynn Shackleford, who were excellent shooters. If Lew was in the clear, he scored himself.

Against Washington State he scored 61 points and broke his own record.

UCLA won twenty-five games in a row and finished the regular season undefeated. They were champions of the Pacific Eight. After the regular season, they played in a big tournament in Louisville, Kentucky. The tournament was run by the National Collegiate Athletic Association (NCAA). The best college teams from all over the country were there.

Most people figured that the

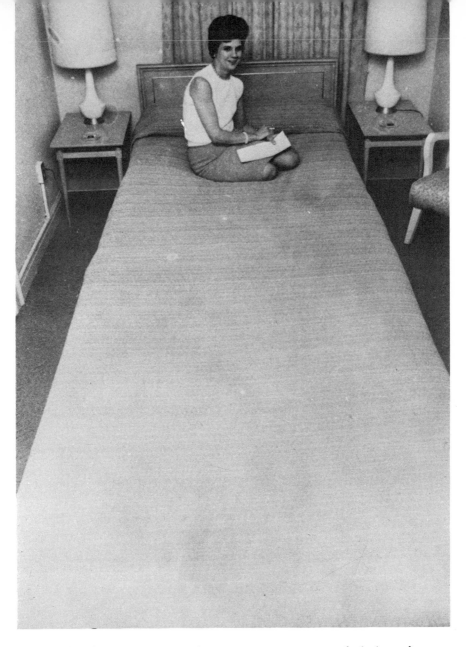

Louisville hotel employee tests out special sleeping
arrangement for Lew: two beds put end to end.

two greatest college players that year were Lew Alcindor and Elvin Hayes. Elvin Hayes was a 6-foot 8-inch center for the University of Houston.

All season long, basketball fans had been waiting for a chance to see the two superstars play against each other. The chance finally came in the NCAA tournament in Louisville when UCLA met Houston.

Lew knew that people would be comparing him to Elvin Hayes. But he didn't care about looking better than Elvin. He just wanted UCLA to win the game.

From the start the Houston players ganged up on him. They guarded him closely and roughly. Under the basket, they pushed and shoved him, hoping to make him mad enough to commit a foul. Five fouls and he would have to leave the game.

Lew kept calm and only fouled twice. When pushing didn't work, the Houston players tried to make him mad by insulting him. Elvin

Hayes told Lew he was going to teach him how to play basketball. Lew kept his cool.

Elvin Hayes ended up making more baskets than Lew. But UCLA won the game by a score of 73–58. For Lew that was what counted.

In the final game of the tournament UCLA trounced Dayton by a score of 79–64. The victory made UCLA the national champions. Lew was named the most valuable player of the tournament.

Out jumping Houston's Hayes.

His first year on the varsity had been a great success. He had scored an average of 29 points a game and grabbed an average of 15 rebounds. He had made two-thirds of all the shots he took, which gave him the best shooting percentage of any college player in history.

Apart from basketball, Lew was still not very happy at UCLA. He often thought about quitting and going to the University of Michigan instead. There were more black students there. He might have a better time. There was just one problem. According to college rules, he would have to sit out one whole basketball season if he switched schools. Reluctantly he decided to stay at UCLA.

That summer he and a couple of professional players from the New York Knickerbockers spent their time visiting poor neighborhoods all over New York City. They showed young boys how to play basketball. They taught them the different shots and

Teaching boys how to shoot.

moves. The job paid well. But
what Lew really liked about it
was the good feeling of being
able to make a lot of kids happy.

# 6

# Alcindor vs. Hayes

In Lew's third year only one
thing stood between the UCLA
basketball team and another
national championship. That was
the University of Houston team,
which was led once again by the
great center Elvin Hayes. Both
teams were undefeated when
they met in Houston part way

through the season for a show-down.

The Houston Astrodome was packed with 52,693 fans. It was the biggest crowd ever to watch a basketball game. Millions more watched the game on TV.

Lew was not up to par. Someone had poked a finger in his left eye in a game the week before. His eyeball was scratched and he was having trouble see-ing. Everything he looked at ap-peared to be blurred. He spent three days resting in bed with a patch over his eye. He was weak

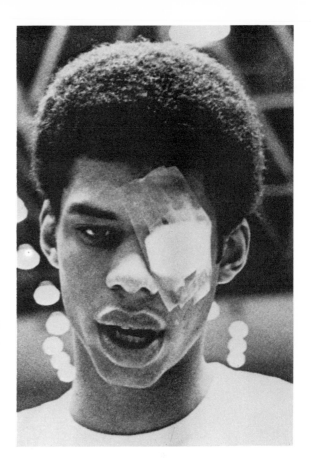

Recovering from a
scratched eyeball.

and out of shape from missing
practice. But he thought the team
needed him and so he played.

He did not play well. His aim
was off because of his eye injury.

He made only 4 out of 18 shots, which was the worst shooting of his career. He also tired fast and was unable to stop Elvin Hayes. Hayes wound up scoring 39 points.

Even though Lew played badly, the game was close. With only 28 seconds to go, the score was tied 69–69. Elvin Hayes stepped to the free-throw line to shoot two foul shots. He made them both. Houston won the game by a score of 71–69.

For UCLA the loss ended a forty-seven-game winning streak.

Afterward, sportswriters said that Houston was the Number One college team in the nation and that UCLA was only second best. Lew Alcindor and his teammates did not agree. They knew they would probably get another chance to play Houston in the NCAA tournament at the end of the season. They could hardly wait for the chance to prove that UCLA was really Number One. As a reminder Lew cut out a magazine cover showing Elvin Hayes scoring against him and pasted it inside his locker.

Lew's eye healed quickly. UCLA won the rest of its games. That spring the showdown the team was waiting for finally came. UCLA met Houston again in Los Angeles in the semifinal round of the NCAA tournament.

The game had just begun when one of the Houston players poked Lew in the ribs and said, "Man, we're gonna beat you! We're gonna beat you bad!" Lew looked around. It was Elvin Hayes.

Elvin's prediction could not have been more wrong. UCLA did such a great job of guarding

Hayes that he was able to score only 10 points and grab only 5 rebounds. Lew meanwhile scored 19 points and pulled down 18 rebounds. The whole UCLA team played like champions. They easily won the game by a score of 101–69.

Lew left the game two minutes and four seconds before it ended. As he walked off the court, the fans stood up and cheered. Lew held up one finger above his head. It meant "We're Number One."

"That was about the greatest

Scoring on a hook shot over Hayes.

exhibition of basketball I've ever seen," said the Houston coach afterward.

Lew felt like celebrating. He went to the locker room and put on a colorful African robe. Then he stepped out into the crowd. The robe was yellow, red and orange, and it came down to his knees. It was so brightly colored that some people thought Lew was trying to show off. Maybe he was — just a little. But, mostly, wearing the robe was a way for him to say, "I'm black and I'm proud of being black.

Here it is, man, you can take it or leave it. This is me!"

UCLA went on to beat North Carolina in the final game of the tournament by a score of 78–55. The UCLA team was the national champion once again.

Lew was so pleased that he took down the net after the game and draped it around his neck. Then for the second year in a row he was given a gold watch for being the tournament's most valuable player. He gave the net and the watch to his mother, Cora, who had come all the way from New York to watch the game.

"I'm very excited," said Mrs. Alcindor. "It's been such a great night for Lew. I think I'm going to have this net made into a turban."

Lew and his happy mother celebrating NCAA championship.

# 7

# Senior Year

The summer before his final year at UCLA, Lew did a lot of thinking. The more he studied the Islamic religion the more sense it made to him. The people who follow the religion are called Muslims. They believe that there is only one God, named Allah, and that men of all colors are brothers.

Lew decided to become a Muslim. When he was baptized, he was given an Islamic name: Kareem Abdul Jabbar, which means "generous and powerful servant of Allah." His close friends called him by the new name. It didn't matter to him that the fans kept right on calling him Lew.

Kareem's religion changed his whole way of thinking. For a long time he had believed that all white people were evil and cruel and that blacks were better human beings. Islam helped him to stop hating whites. It taught him to believe that all men are brothers and that no race of people is better or worse than any other.

In his senior year the UCLA team was rolling toward an un-defeated season when it came up against the University of Southern California. The USC team tried to slow down the game. Instead of taking a lot of shots they held onto the ball for as long as possible. The strategy worked. USC upset UCLA by the unusually low score of 46–44.

That was UCLA's only loss of

Watching USC make the winning basket.

the year. After the regular season ended, they played in the NCAA tournament once again. They beat the team from Drake University by a score of 85–82 in the semifinal round. Then they played Purdue for the championship.

It was Lew's last college game. His father did something he had been wanting to do for a long time. He sat behind the bench and played trombone with the UCLA band. With Mr. Alcindor rooting him on, Lew played a great game. He scored 37 points and grabbed 20 rebounds. UCLA won by a score of 92–72.

Lew's amazing college career was over. With him leading the team, UCLA won eighty-eight games and lost only twice, once to Houston and once to USC. They won three NCAA championships in a row, something no other team has ever been able to do. Lew won the award for being the tournament's most valuable player three times in a row, and that is something no other player has ever been able to do. In his three varsity seasons he scored a total of 2,325 points and made 1,367 rebounds. He was one of the biggest and best college basketball players anybody had ever seen. It was no wonder that he was the Number One choice of every professional basketball team.

Graduating from college.

# 8

# Joining the Bucks

On April 2, 1969, shortly before he was graduated from UCLA, Lew signed a contract to play professional basketball with the Milwaukee Bucks. The Bucks were a new team in the National Basketball Association. In their first year in the league they had finished last. They needed a good big man to play center. Lew Alcindor was the perfect man for the job.

The Bucks agreed to pay Lew $1,400,000 to play for five years. That was the most money that had ever been offered to a basketball player. In fact, it was the most money that had ever been offered to any athlete in any sport. It made Lew an instant millionaire at the age of twenty-two. He was the first player ever to become a millionaire just by turning pro.

He didn't let his sudden wealth go to his head. He bought some new clothes because his old ones

Signing his contract with Milwaukee.

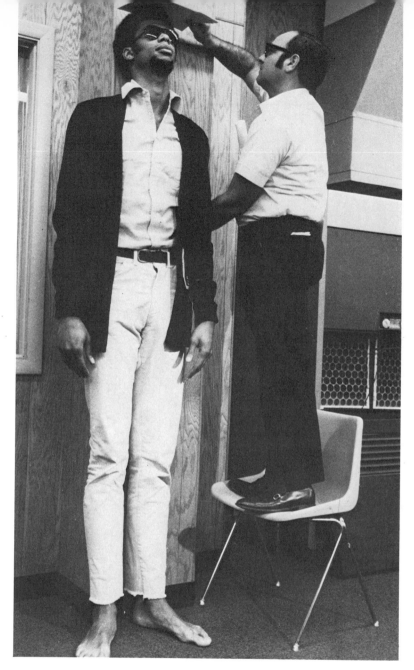

Being measured by Milwaukee trainer.

were wearing out. He needed a car that was big enough for him, so he bought a Cadillac. He also bought a set of drums.

When he arrived at the Milwaukee Bucks training camp, he weighed in at 230 pounds and stood 7 feet 1⅝ inches tall. The trainer had to stand on a chair to measure him.

Trying on his pro uniform.

The Milwaukee fans were hoping that the giant rookie center would turn the Bucks around. With Big Lew leading the team, maybe they could finish first.

The Bucks got off to a good start. They won their first three games easily. Then they flew to California to play the Los Angeles Lakers. It was a game that everyone had been waiting for. Facing Lew at center for the Lakers was Wilt Chamberlain, the strongest man in basketball.

Wilt was about as tall as Lew

and 50 pounds heavier, but Lew managed to hold his own. He wasn't as strong, but he was quicker. He scored 23 points and made 20 rebounds. Wilt scored 25 points and made 25 rebounds. The Bucks lost to the Lakers by a score of 123–112.

Lew learned that there is a big difference between the way pro teams and college teams play basketball. He found out that the pro game is not only much faster but also much rougher. Other players were pushing and shoving him and hitting him with

Alcindor and Chamberlain bump hard.

their elbows when the referees weren't looking.

It bothered him. "This contact is new to me, and I'm still learning to cope with it," he said.

One night he was being pushed around by Bob Rule, a 6-foot 9-inch center for the Seattle Supersonics. When Rule stuck a finger in his eye, Lew decided that he had taken enough. He charged at Rule. The fight was quickly stopped, but Lew had made his point.

"It's going to be rough for me, but I might make it just as rough for them," he said afterward. "It works both ways, you know."

In his very first season as a pro Lew proved that he was a superstar. He scored an average of 28.8 points a game and was the league's second highest scorer. Only Jerry West of the Los Angeles Lakers scored more. Lew was also good at blocking shots, grabbing rebounds, and passing the ball off to teammates for baskets. He led Milwaukee to a second-place finish. He was named Rookie of the Year.

# 9

# 1970 Play-offs

After the regular season, the Bucks entered the play-offs for the National Basketball Association championship. In the first round of the play-offs they met the Philadelphia 76'ers. Lew was unstoppable. He scored an average of 36 points a game and the Bucks beat the 76'ers four games out of five.

Blocking a shot
by Philadelphia's
Dennis Awtrey.

In the next round the Bucks
played the New York Knicks.
The Knicks were a great team.
They were all good shooters, and
they also played tough defense.
They were led by Willis Reed,
their star center. Willis was five

inches shorter than Lew, but he was stronger and more solidly built. He was the league's most valuable player that year.

The series opened in Madison Square Garden in New York. At first both the Knicks and the Bucks were nervous. The players had trouble holding onto the ball. They made a lot of wild passes. After a while they settled down.

Lew played a fine game. He scored 35 points, which was 11 points more than Willis Reed scored. But the rest of the Knicks outshot the Bucks, and Milwaukee lost the game by a score of 110–102.

In the second game Lew was doing just as well — up until the last minute. He had scored 36 points and grabbed 23 rebounds. The game was very close. The Bucks were trailing, but by only one point. Then, with 52 seconds left, Lew was fouled. He walked to the free-throw line to try two shots. If he had made them both, the Bucks might have won by a point. Instead, he missed them both and the Bucks lost by a point.

It must have embarrassed Lew terribly to miss those foul shots. To get himself into a good mood for the third game, he listened to some jazz. Just before the game he stood still on the court and collected his thoughts.

He played a tremendous game. He scored 33 points and made 31 rebounds. The whole Knick team made only 42 rebounds combined. The Bucks won the game by a score of 101–96.

The Milwaukee coach, Larry Costello, said it was the best game Lew had ever played.

"There's really not much you can do to stop him," said Willis Reed. "Just hope he's not shooting well. If he gets position, he's going to score."

Scoring on a jump shot over New York's Reed.

The next game was very important for the Bucks. If they won it, they would even the series at two victories for each team. If they lost, they would drop behind three games to one. Lew scored 38 points, but he made only 9 rebounds. The Bucks lost by a score of 117–105. One more loss and they would be out of the play-offs.

Good as Alcindor was, the Knicks were a better team than the Bucks. The New Yorkers proved just how much better they were in the final game of the series. Lew scored 27 points in the game, but it was not nearly enough. New York demolished Milwaukee by a score of 132–96.

At the end of the game some of the New York fans started a sarcastic chant. "Good-bye, Lewie!" they yelled. Lew didn't let the rude fans get him down. He knew that in another year the Milwaukee Bucks would probably have another chance for the championship. Then things might turn out differently.

# 10

# World Champions

After the 1970 play-offs the Bucks made a great trade. They got Oscar Robertson, an All-Star guard, from the Cincinnati Royals. Oscar was one of the league's best players. He was a slick ball handler and a fine shooter. He could really move a team.

The Alcindor-Robertson combination worked. In Lew's second year as a pro the Bucks were seldom beaten. At one point they won twenty games in a row. That set the league record for consecutive victories. They finished the season first in their division.

Lew led the league in scoring with an average of more than 31 points a game. But as much as possible he liked to share the scoring with his teammates. He was good at hitting them with passes for baskets. He was voted the most valuable player in the league.

In the first round of the 1971 play-offs the Milwaukee Bucks beat the San Francisco Warriors four games out of five. Then they beat the Los Angeles Lakers four out of five and entered the final play-off round for the National Basketball Association championship.

The Bucks were hoping for a chance to get even with the New York Knicks in the finals. But the Baltimore Bullets upset the Knicks in the semifinal round and earned the right to play Milwaukee for the championship.

The Bullets were a fine team, but two of their star players, forward Gus Johnson and guard Kevin Loughery, were sidelined with injuries. Baltimore's center, Westley Unseld, stood only 6 feet 5 inches and was simply no match for Big Lew.

Milwaukee trounced Baltimore in four straight games. Lew led the team in scoring. He also led the defense in blocking shots.

The Bucks were champions of the world. The title made Lew

Lew bats ball back in the face of Baltimore shooters.

feel very proud. Later he was
voted the most valuable player in
the play-offs. That made him feel
proud, too.

Honor followed honor. The United States government asked Lew if he would like to make a tour of Africa. He quickly agreed.

Before he went, Lew took two big steps. He decided to change his name legally to Kareem Abdul Jabbar. And he married a Muslim girl named Habiba.

Kareem

Habiba

Mr. and Mrs. Jabbar made the trip to Africa together. Kareem was excited as he boarded the plane. Visiting the land of his ancestors was something he had dreamed of doing for a long time.

## The Authors

Marshall and Sue Burchard are married and the parents of two children, Marshall and Wendy. They live in New York City but have spent the past few summers in Spain. Marshall, a former education editor of *Time* magazine, is presently a free-lance writer. Sue is a librarian at Trinity School. Their previous books for Putnam's were *Sport's Hero: Joe Namath* and *Brooks Robinson: Sports Hero*.